WYNTON MARSALIS
Gifted Trumpet Player

By Craig Awmiller

CHILDREN'S PRESS ®
A Division of Grolier Publishing
New York / London / Hong Kong / Sydney
Danbury, Connecticut

DEDICATION
_____

To Neil Smith, music teacher

PHOTO CREDITS
_____

Cover: Gamma-Liaison Network (Arnaldo Magnani)
Retna Ltd.: title page (Andy Freeberg), pp. 13 (David
    Redfern), 15 (Veryl Oakland), 16 (Gary Gershoff),
    22 right (William Gottlieb)
Stephanie Berger: pp. 3, 5, 26, 28, 31
AP/Wide World Photos: pp. 7, 24, 27, 32 top right
NOCCA: p. 10
The Juilliard School: p. 11 (Janet Kessin)
UPI/Bettmann: pp. 18, 20 right
W. P. Gottlieb. Library of Congress/Gershwin Fund:
    p. 20 left, 22 left
Gamma-Liaison Network: pp. 23 (both Alain
    Benainous)

EDITORIAL STAFF
_____

Project Editor: Sarah DeCapua
Design and Electronic Composition: Biner Design
Photo Editor: Caroline Anderson

Library of Congress Cataloging-in-Publication Data
Awmiller, Craig.
    Wynton Marsalis / by Craig Awmiller.
        p.   cm. — (A picture-story biography)
        ISBN 0-516-04196-7
        1. Marsalis, Wynton, 1961-   —Juvenile literature. 2.
Trumpet players—United States—Biography—Juvenile
literature. [1. Marsalis, Wynton, 1961- . 2. Trumpet
players. 3. Musicians. 4. Afro-Americans—Biography.] I.
Title. II. Series : Picture story biographies.
ML3930.M327A96   1996
788.9 ' 2 ' 092—dc20
[B]   95-51027
CIP
                                                          AC   MN

THE MOST FAMOUS trumpet player in the world steps out onto the stage. His name is Wynton Marsalis. He stands next to the microphone and waves at all the people who have come to hear him play.

"Good evening, ladies and gentlemen," he says. "Thank you for coming out tonight. We hope you enjoy yourselves. Because we are here to swing."

With that, Wynton puts his trumpet to his lips. For the next three hours, the audience will listen to the wonderful music that Wynton and his band play so well. Some of the songs are fast. Some are slow. Some songs sound happy. Others sound sad. But, one way or another, all of them are beautiful.

When the concert is over, the audience stands up and claps. They whistle and cheer. Everyone loves what they heard. Just as Wynton had hoped, they have all enjoyed themselves.

But the night is not over for Wynton. A group of children is waiting for him backstage. All of the children have musical instruments. After his concerts, Wynton gives music lessons to children who want to learn how to play their instruments better. Wynton loves playing music for an audience, but teaching children about music is Wynton's favorite part of the night.

Wynton demonstrates his technique to music students.

"Do you have something you want me to hear?" Wynton asks a serious-looking boy who is holding a trumpet.

"Yes I do, Mr. Marsalis," the boy says.

"Just call me Wynton. Now let's hear what you have."

The boy smiles and begins playing his horn. Wynton listens carefully. He knows how important it is for children to be given encouragement. Learning to play an instrument takes patience.

Sometimes it can be very hard. So it means a lot to be encouraged by such a famous musician. Wynton wants all the children he teaches to know that when he first started playing the trumpet, he couldn't play it very well at all. But now, thanks to years of practice, he plays the trumpet better than almost anyone else.

Wynton was born on October 18, 1961, in New Orleans, Louisiana. The house where he grew up was filled with music. His father, Ellis Marsalis, played the piano. His older brother, Branford, played the saxophone. His younger brother, Delfaeyo, played the trombone. His youngest brother, Jason, played the drums. With so many musicians living there, music could be heard at the Marsalis house at any time of day. One of the Marsalis brothers might be in the kitchen, blowing his

Wynton (right) with brother Branford (left) and father Ellis (middle)

horn. Another would be in an upstairs bedroom, practicing scales on his saxophone. Meanwhile, their father might be writing a song on the piano in the living room. Even though she didn't play an instrument herself, Delores Marsalis, Wynton's mother, never got tired of listening to all this music. She encouraged all her sons to be musicians. She wanted them to play the best that they could.

"My mother put a tremendous investment of her time in our development," Wynton says. "She took us to music camps, taught us the importance of culture, gave us books to read. She had a powerful influence."

Wynton's mother helped him in other ways, too. Like most kids, Wynton sometimes got into trouble. But his mother made sure he concentrated on his music and not on getting into trouble.

"When I was twelve," Wynton says, "I thought it was cool to be hanging out on the street. I was stealing stuff. Fighting. A neighbor told my mama about this and my mama took me out in the street and paddled my behind in front of my friends. I had to stay inside for awhile after that, because that blew my cool in the neighborhood."

His bottom still a little sore, Wynton decided it would be better to keep out of mischief, and to go on learning to play the trumpet.

But playing the trumpet wasn't always easy for Wynton. He had to work very hard. Sometimes his playing didn't sound good at all. Sometimes instead of playing a note of music, he would make a mistake and his trumpet would let out a funny sound. The sound was like a goose honking, or a duck quacking. It did not sound like a trumpet at all. Wynton didn't like it when this happened, so he tried not to make mistakes.

When Wynton tried out for his high school band, he almost wasn't allowed to join. The teacher thought the music the band played might be too difficult for Wynton. The teacher knew that Wynton's father was a very good piano player. But Wynton didn't seem to have any of his father's talent. Still, Wynton promised that he would try even harder

From an early age, Wynton worked hard to learn the trumpet. Here, he plays in the New Orleans Center for Creative Arts Festival Brass Quartet (1978).

to improve his playing. Finally, the teacher let him join the band.

Wynton kept his promise. He learned as much about music as he could. He practiced his trumpet for hours every day. When everyone else in the house had gone to sleep, Wynton would go outside to practice. Standing out under the stars, Wynton would play until he was too tired to stand up any more. He loved music more than anything else in the world. He played every chance he got.

Finally, the results of Wynton's hard work started to show. By the time he finished high school, Wynton had become a very good trumpet player. He was so good that his mother, father, and band teacher thought he should go to the Juilliard School of Music. The Juilliard School of Music is in New York City. It is the most famous music school in the world. It is a special kind of

The Juilliard School in New York City, where Wynton studied music

school because only a few students are allowed to go there each year. A person must be an excellent musician to be able to go to Juilliard. The teachers there all thought Wynton was talented enough to come to their school.

Once at Juilliard, Wynton still had to work very hard. All day long he took classes about music and practiced his trumpet. At night, to earn money, he played in a band that performed the music for a Broadway play. With all this work, he was often very tired. But being at Juilliard was fun, too. Wynton was meeting people from all over the world who loved music as much as he did. The best thing of all, though, was that he was becoming an even better trumpet player.

The teachers at the school were quite impressed with Wynton. They thought he was one of the best trumpet players to have ever gone to the school.

Another person who was impressed with Wynton was a man named Art Blakey. Art Blakey was a famous drummer who had his own band. It was called "The Jazz Messengers." He asked Wynton to join the band. Wynton could barely believe his ears! It was a dream come true to play in a band as well known as Art Blakey's. So Wynton packed up his trumpet and started traveling with the Jazz Messengers as they went all over the country, playing their music.

Art Blakey encouraged Wynton to form his own band.

Everywhere the band went, the audience loved the way Wynton played the trumpet. He was so good! People said they had never heard someone play the trumpet that well! Art Blakey was even more impressed with Wynton than he had been before. He thought that Wynton should have his own band. At first, Wynton wasn't sure if Art Blakey was right. He didn't think he was good enough to have his own band. But Art Blakey thought so. And so did some people at a record company, who wanted Wynton to record music for them. They wanted to put out a record that featured Wynton playing the trumpet.

Wynton was amazed when he thought about how far he'd come. It had only been three years since he left home for New York City, and now he had his own band and his first record coming out.

Wynton (left) formed a quartet in 1982 with Tony Williams, Ron Carter, and Herbie Hancock.

That was in 1982. Since then, Wynton has never stopped playing music, making records, and touring the country with his band. He has played music with many other famous musicians. Many of the musicians in his band have become famous themselves. Sometimes the other musicians in his band have a hard time keeping up with Wynton. Wynton loves music so much that he works almost all the time. He never seems to rest. "I'm always practicing. I never take a break. I have played the trumpet almost every night for the last fifteen years," Wynton says.

You can tell Wynton works hard when you look at all the records he has made. Since he made his first record, Wynton has made thirty more. Imagine making more than thirty records!

Wynton (second from right) and his bands have always been known for their hard work and dedication.

Whenever he is not touring the country with his band, Wynton can probably be found in a recording studio.

Wynton has made two different kinds of records. He is most famous for making "jazz" records. But Wynton has also made records that are called "classical." Classical music was invented in Europe hundreds of years ago. Some of the most well known classical composers are Beethoven, Mozart, and Brahms.

Most trumpet players play either classical music or jazz music. Classical and jazz are very different from each other. Both can be hard to play, so most trumpet players only concentrate on playing one of them very well.

Wynton, though, is such a good trumpet player that he can play both classical and jazz music. No one else in the world can play both kinds of music as well as Wynton can play them.

Over the years, Wynton's records have won many awards. The most famous award he has won is called the "Grammy." Wynton won a Grammy award for his very first jazz record. Since then he has won many more. In 1984, Wynton was the first person in history to win two Grammy awards in the same

Wynton accepts the 1984 Grammy award for Best Jazz Album.

year—one for playing classical music and one for playing jazz music. The following year, Wynton won the same awards. No one else had ever won these awards two years in a row.

And because he never stopped working hard, Wynton is now the most famous trumpet player in the world.

———⟶⟶●⟵⟵———

Wynton's favorite kind of music is jazz. Jazz music was invented by African-Americans about one hundred years ago. The instruments that are most often used to play jazz are the trumpet, the saxophone, the piano, the string bass, and the drums. Some famous jazz musicians are Louis Armstrong, Duke Ellington, and Count Basie. Other famous jazz musicians include Charlie Parker, Miles Davis, and Dizzy Gillespie.

When Wynton teaches children about jazz, he explains the two things in particular that make jazz special.

The first is called *rhythm*.

The second is called *improvisation*.

Rhythm is the "beat" behind all the music. Wynton encourages listeners to clap their hands along to the music being played. It usually sounds better if the clapping is done in a steady, regular way.

Louis Armstrong (left) and Duke Ellington (right) were famous jazz musicians who influenced Wynton Marsalis.

In jazz, the drummer is in charge of playing the rhythm. He or she plays a steady pattern on the drums. All the other musicians in the band pay close attention to the drummer. They listen to the steady pattern being played. They make sure they follow along with the rhythm of the music.

Improvisation is just a big word that means "making something up as you go along." When jazz musicians are playing together, they don't always know exactly what they are going to play. They might have a general idea, but they leave places in the music where the musician can play anything he or she wants to play.

Instead of knowing what music is going to be played, the musician makes it up at the same time the audience is listening! It takes courage for a musician to improvise.

When Wynton's band is playing, there are usually times when all the musicians play quietly. Sometimes the band stops playing altogether. Wynton, though, keeps playing. When he is playing by himself like this, it is called playing a "solo." Most of the time when Wynton starts to play a solo, he doesn't know exactly what he is going

to play. Instead, he improvises. He remembers what the other musicians have been playing, and he makes up something that goes along with it. Wynton is considered especially good at improvising.

All the members of the band take turns doing a solo. With each solo, the musician improvises something new.

Wynton Marsalis has become as well known as Count Basie (opposite page, left), Charlie Parker (opposite page, right), Miles Davis (left), and Dizzy Gillespie (below). They were some of the most famous jazz musicians in history.

Each musician plays his or her solo in a different way—fast, slow, loud, or soft. Some musicians play for a long time. Some play for just a little while. As long as the music each person is playing sounds good, the band members can play whatever they want.

Today, Wynton lives in an apartment in New York City. When he and his band travel across the country, they ride in a big bus. Everywhere they stop, they play music. When they go to some far away

Wynton (left) directs band members in practice.

place, they ride in a plane. Together, Wynton and his band have gone all over the world. No matter where he goes, though, Wynton plays his music the best that he can. He also likes to make friends wherever he goes.

In the past few years, Wynton has started to write his own music. Ideas for music come to him at all sorts of times. Sometimes, an idea will come as he is walking along the sidewalk. Other times, an idea might come to him in a dream. Or, he might be riding with everyone else in the big bus when an idea comes to him. Whenever he "hears" some music in his head that he wants to remember, Wynton will grab some paper and a pen and write down the idea.

"Music comes to you at strange times," Wynton says, "but you have to be ready to catch it, because if you don't she may be gone for good."

Wynton gives different names to each piece of music he writes. Some of the names of Wynton's music are *Citi Movement*, *In This House*, *On this Morning*, and *Blood on the Fields*.

Another job Wynton has is at Lincoln Center for the Performing Arts in New York City. Lincoln Center is a world-famous place where performers put on plays, operas, and different kinds of music. Wynton's job at Lincoln Center is to put programs about jazz music together. He has been doing this since 1991.

Lincoln Center is world famous for the great performances that take place there.

Leonard Bernstein inspired Wynton to teach children about music.

The programs are designed to teach people more about jazz. Wynton was inspired in this job by a classical composer and conductor named Leonard Bernstein, who died in 1990. When he was alive, Leonard Bernstein put programs together that taught children and young people about classical music. He taught all about the different instruments and how to play them.

Wynton (left) dribbles a basketball to demonstrate the principle of rhythm.

Today, Wynton does the same thing that Leonard Bernstein did. Except Wynton teaches children about jazz. He teaches them how it got started, about the famous men and women who played it, and how a jazz band works together to make good music. He also tells the children about the importance of rhythm and improvisation.

Wynton also travels throughout the country, visiting many different schools and teaching children about jazz. Everywhere he goes, he tries to make sure that children are learning about music in their schools.

And everywhere he goes, he tells children that if they want to be good musicians, they have to do one thing more than anything else—practice.

Wynton says, "Kids always ask, 'Man, how were you discovered?' and I say, 'Man, when I discovered the practice room.' You won't get nowhere without sweat."

And that is just what he says backstage, after the concert, to the serious-looking boy who is holding the trumpet.

"So if you want to get better," Wynton tells him, "you need to practice every day."

The boy looks a little sad. He was hoping that Wynton would tell him a magic secret that would make playing the trumpet easy.

Wynton sees that the boy was hoping to hear something else. "That's the only way," Wynton says. "If you really love music, that's what you'll do."

The boy looks up at Wynton.

"And then, maybe, I'll be as good as you are?" the boy asks.

"And then you'll be as good as me," Wynton says.

The boy smiles. He and Wynton shake hands.

Next in line is a girl holding a saxophone. Behind her is another boy holding a trumpet. They are all looking forward to their own personal lesson with Wynton.

Wynton looks at all the children. He smiles at them.

It looks like Wynton is going to be here all night doing what he loves the most—teaching children about music.

No matter how hard Wynton works, he always makes time to give pointers to young musicians.

Wynton Marsalis

1961   October 18—Wynton Marsalis is born in New Orleans, Louisiana

1967   Given first trumpet

1969   Joins marching band, which performs at New Orleans Jazz and Heritage Festival

1975   Performs with New Orleans Philharmonic Orchestra

1979   Enters the Juilliard School of Music in New York City

1980   Joins Art Blakey's Jazz Messengers

1981   Releases first album, *Wynton Marsalis*

1982   Forms quintet with his brother, Branford

1983   Wins Grammy award for his jazz album, *Think of One*

1984   Wins two Grammy awards: one for his jazz music and one for his classical music

1986   Forms the Wynton Marsalis Quartet

1991   Becomes the director of the Jazz Program at Lincoln Center

1992   Forms the Wynton Marsalis Septet

1994   Publishes a book about jazz music called, *Sweet Swing Blues on the Road*

1995   Airs his PBS series, *Marsalis on Music*

Index

About the Author

Craig Awmiller is a writer and musician whose first book, *This House on Fire: The Story of the Blues* was published by Franklin Watts. *Wynton Marsalis: Gifted Trumpet Player* is his first book for Children's Press. Mr. Awmiller lives in Tacoma, Washington, with his wife, Shelly, and their cat, Lily.